Project Editors: Joy Marple & Cara Bailey
Designers: Patti Matthews & Mark Veldheer
Illustration: Robin Moro

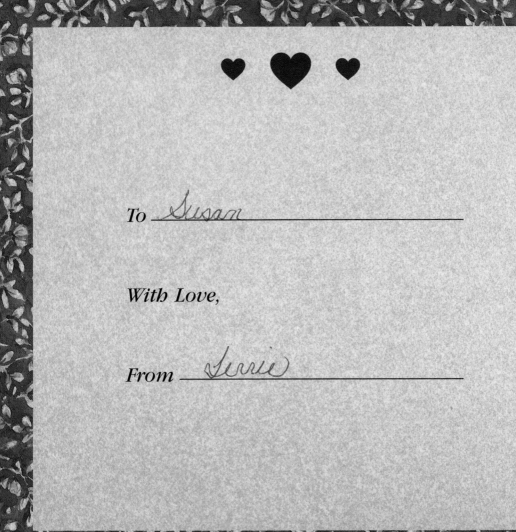

To _Susan_

With Love,

From _Terrie_

Love

I love you,
Not only for what you are,
But for what I am
When I am with you.

I love you,
Not only for what
You have made of yourself,
But for what
You are making of me.

I love you
For the part of me
That you bring out.

Roy Croft

Be completely humble and gentle; be patient,
bearing with one another in love.

Ephesians 4:2

A man of many companions may come to ruin,
but there is a friend who sticks closer than a brother.

Proverbs 18:24

Lord, make me an instrument of your peace; where there is
hatred, let me sow love; where there is injury, pardon; where
there is doubt, faith; where there is despair, hope; where there
is darkness, light; and where there is sadness, joy.

St. Francis of Assisi

Therefore, as God's chosen people, holy and dearly loved,
clothe yourselves with compassion, kindness, humility,
gentleness and patience. Bear with each other. . .

Colossians 3:12-13

Love looks not with the eyes, but with the mind.

William Shakespeare from
A Midsummer Night's Dream

Praise be to the LORD, to God our Savior,
who daily bears our burdens.

Psalm 68:19

He whose hand is clasped in friendship cannot throw mud.

Anonymous

Love is patient, love is kind. It does not envy, it does not boast, it is not proud. It is not rude, it is not self-seeking, it is not easily angered, it keeps no record of wrongs. Love does not delight in evil but rejoices with the truth. It always protects, always trusts, always hopes, always perseveres. Love never fails.

1 Corinthians 13:4-8a

Do not forsake your friend and the friend of your father.

Proverbs 27:10

Love feels no burdens,
thinks nothing of trouble,
attempts what is above its strength,
pleads no excuse of impractibility—
for it thinks all things lawful
for itself if possible.

Thomas a Kempis

So long as we love, we serve; so long as we are loved by
others, I should say that we are almost indispensable;
and no man is useless while he has a friend.

Robert Louis Stevenson

It brings comfort to have companions in whatever happens.

Saint John Chrysostom

Love is a good above all others, which alone
maketh every burden light.
Love is watchful, and whilst sleeping still keeps watch;
though fatigued is not weary; though pressed is not forced.
Love is sincere, gentle, strong, patient, faithful,
prudent, long-suffering, manly.
Love is circumspect, humble, upright; not weary, not fickle,
nor intent on vain things; sober, chaste, steadfast,
quiet, and guarded in all the senses.

Thomas a Kempis

A friend is one to whom one may pour out all the contents of one's heart, chaff and grain together, knowing that the gentlest of hands will take and sift it, keep what is worth keeping, and with a breath of kindness, blow the rest away.

Anonymous

The best portion of a good man's life is his little, nameless, unremembered acts of kindness and of love.

William Wordsworth

Happiness is a perfume you cannot pour on others without getting a few drops on yourself.

Anonymous

There never was any heart truly great and generous,
that was not also tender and compassionate.

Robert Frost

God is love. Whoever lives in love lives in God, and God in him.
There is no fear in love.

1 John 4:16b,18a

An acquaintance that begins with a compliment is sure
to develop into a real friendship.

Oscar Wilde

"A new command I give you: Love one another. As I have loved you, so you must love one another. By this all men will know that you are my disciples, if you love one another."

John 13:34-35

What is a friend? A single soul dwelling in two bodies.

Aristotle

We love because he first loved us. And he has given us this command: Whoever loves God must also love his brother.

1 John 4:19, 21

May the Lord make your love increase and overflow
for each other and for everyone else.

1 Thessalonians 3:12

A friendship like love is warm; A love like friendship steady.

Thomas Moore

There is nothing more valuable to give a friend
than a silent prayer on their behalf.

A friend loves at all times.

Proverbs 17:17

Grant that I may not so much seek to be consoled as to console;
to be understood as to understand; to be loved as to love; for it
is in giving that we receive, it is in pardoning that we are
pardoned, and it is in dying that we are born to eternal life.
Amen.

St. Francis of Assisi

Love must be sincere. Hate what is evil; cling to
what is good. Be devoted to one another in brotherly love.
Honor one another above yourselves.

Romans 12:9-10

A friend is a present which you give yourself.

Robert Louis Stevenson

Do everything in love.

1 Corinthians 16:14

I hold it true, whate'er befall;
I feel it, when I sorrow most;
'Tis better to have loved and lost
Than never to have loved at all.

Alfred, Lord Tennyson

Blest be the tie that binds
Our hearts in Christian love;
The fellowship of kindred minds,
Is like to that above.

John Fawcett

Friendship is celebrating each other's successes
and bearing each other's burdens.

Love is encouraging when you're discouraged—rejoicing
when you're troubled—comforting when you're distressed.

Let us not love with words or tongue but with actions and in truth.

1 John 3:18

Friend: one who knows all about you and loves you just the same.

Elbert Hubbard

Dear friends, let us love one another, for love comes from God.
Since God so loved us, we also ought to love one another.

1 John 4:7a, 11

Your love has given me great joy and encouragement.

Philemon 7

If you want a person's faults, go to those who love him.
They will not tell you, but they know.

Robert Louis Stevenson

God is love. Whoever lives in love lives in God, and God in him. In this way, love is made complete among us so that we will have confidence on the day of judgment, because in this world we are like him. There is no fear in love.

1 John 4:16b–18a

The Love of God

All things that are on earth shall wholly pass away,
Except the love of God, which shall live and last for aye.
The forms of men shall be as they had never been;
And realms shall be dissolved, and empires be no more.

Bernard Rascas

A friend is one before whom I may think aloud.

Ralph Waldo Emerson

That I did always love,
I bring thee proof:
That till I loved I did not love enough.

That I shall love always,
I offer thee
That love is life,
And life hath immortality.

This, dost thou doubt, sweet?
Then have I
Nothing to show
But Calvary.

Emily Dickinson

Thee will I love, O Lord, with all my heart's delight.

Philip Sidney

Love must grow. It can't stand still, and it certainly cannot go
backward. Love must flourish or else it withers and dies.

Joni Eareckson Tada

Warm and lovely memories have a way of helping you
live life better in the present.

Your love, O LORD, endures forever.

Psalm 138:8

Pleasurable things give delight and satisfaction to the soul. Pleasure is found lying under an oak tree, with the cool grass beneath and the rustle of leaves above. Pleasure is sitting by a cheery fire, curled up on the couch with your favorite blanket and cup of tea. Pleasure is captured in the soft smile and gentle eyes of the one you love.

The LORD will take delight in you. . . as a bridegroom rejoices over his bride, so will your God rejoice over you.

Isaiah 62:4b–5

Love is not love
Which alters when it alteration finds.

William Shakespeare

Above all, love each other deeply.

1 Peter 4:8

The God of love my shepherd is,
And he that doth me feed:
While he is mine, and I am his,
What can I want or need?

Surely thy sweet and wondrous love
Shall measure all my days;
And as it never shall remove,
So neither shall my praise.

George Herbert

God's love may be divided up for an infinite number of people on earth, but because His love is eternal and without end, He can still infinitely pour out His love on you.

Joni Eareckson Tada

That Love is all there is,
Is all we know of Love.

Emily Dickinson

We cannot tell the precise moment when friendship is formed. As in filling a vessel drop by drop, there is at last a drop which makes it run over, so in a series of kindnesses there is a last one that makes the heart run over.

Samuel Johnson

Give thanks to the LORD, for he is good. His love endures forever.

Psalm 136:1

The people of God who bind themselves in love are strikingly beautiful. And the world cannot help but be attracted to it.

Joni Eareckson Tada

He prayeth best, who loveth best
All things both great and small;
For the dear God who loveth us,
He made and loveth all.

Samuel T. Coleridge

I tell you there is one thing that draws above everything
else in the world and that is love.

D.L. Moody

The LORD is compassionate and gracious,
    slow to anger, abounding in love.
He will not always accuse,
    nor will he harbor his anger forever;
he does not treat us as our sins deserve
    or repay us according to our iniquities.
For as high as the heavens are above the earth,
    so great is his love for those who fear him. . . .
From everlasting to everlasting
    the LORD's love is with those who fear him. . . .

Psalm 103:8–11, 17

O, 'tis love, 'tis love, that makes the world go round!

Lewis Carroll

For the LORD is good, and his love endures forever;
his faithfulness continues through all generations.

Psalm 100:5

Respect is what we owe; love, what we give.

Philip James Bailey

A sorrow shared is half a trouble,
but a joy that's shared is a joy made double.

English Proverb

Hail guest! We ask not what thou art:
If Friend, we greet thee, hand and heart;
If Stranger, such no longer be;
If Foe, our love shall conquer thee.

Old Welsh Doorpost Welcome

May the Lord make your love increase and overflow for each other
and for everyone else.

1 Thessalonians 3:12

If love could be measured, it would be measured by how
much it gives.

Joni Eareckson Tada

A true friend gives freely, advises justly, assists readily,
adventures boldly, takes all patiently, defends courageously,
and continues a friend unchangeable.

William Penn

To God be humble, to thy friend be kind,
And with thy neighbour, gladly lend and borrow;
His chance tonight, it may be thine tomorrow.

William Dunbar

True love's the gift which God has given
To man alone beneath the heaven.

Sir Walter Scott

The earth is filled with your love, O LORD.

Psalm 119:64

Savior, teach me, day by day,
Love's sweet lesson, to obey;
Sweeter lesson cannot be,
Loving Him who first loved me.

Jane E. Leeson

There never was any heart truly great and generous,
that was not also tender and compassionate.

Robert Frost

If you want to be loved, be lovable.

Ovid

Be a friend to thyself, and others will be so too.

Thomas Fuller

And let us consider how we may spur one another on
toward love and good deeds.

Hebrews 10:24

A friend's embrace brings warmth to your life.

All good gifts around us,
Are sent from heaven above:
Thank the Lord, O thank the Lord,
For all His love.

Mathias Claudias

From the fullness of his grace we have all received one
blessing after another.

John 1:16

Delight yourself in the LORD
and he will give you the desires of your heart.

Psalm 37:4

Blessings abound—look around you. The smiles of children, the
beauty of a glorious sunset, the comfort of a warm bed at night.
Small and great, there are plenty of reasons to say to God,
"Thank you."

Joni Eareckson Tada